MIGHTY MACHINES IN ACTION

Earth Movers

by Rebecca Pettiford

BLASTOFF! READERS
2

BELLWETHER MEDIA • MINNEAPOLIS, MN

Note to Librarians, Teachers, and Parents:

Blastoff! Readers are carefully developed by literacy experts and combine standards-based content with developmentally appropriate text.

Level 1 provides the most support through repetition of high-frequency words, light text, predictable sentence patterns, and strong visual support.

Level 2 offers early readers a bit more challenge through varied simple sentences, increased text load, and less repetition of high-frequency words.

Level 3 advances early-fluent readers toward fluency through increased text and concept load, less reliance on visuals, longer sentences, and more literary language.

Level 4 builds reading stamina by providing more text per page, increased use of punctuation, greater variation in sentence patterns, and increasingly challenging vocabulary.

Level 5 encourages children to move from "learning to read" to "reading to learn" by providing even more text, varied writing styles, and less familiar topics.

Whichever book is right for your reader, Blastoff! Readers are the perfect books to build confidence and encourage a love of reading that will last a lifetime!

This edition first published in 2018 by Bellwether Media, Inc.

No part of this publication may be reproduced in whole or in part without written permission of the publisher. For information regarding permission, write to Bellwether Media, Inc., Attention: Permissions Department, 5357 Penn Avenue South, Minneapolis, MN 55419.

Library of Congress Cataloging-in-Publication Data

Names: Pettiford, Rebecca, author.
Title: Earth Movers / by Rebecca Pettiford.
Description: Minneapolis, MN : Bellwether Media, Inc., [2018] | Series: Blastoff! Readers. Mighty Machines in Action | Includes bibliographical references and index. | Audience: Grades K-3. | Audience: Ages 5-8.
Identifiers: LCCN 2016052742 (print) | LCCN 2016054498 (ebook) | ISBN 9781626176317 (hardcover : alk. paper) | ISBN 9781681033617 (ebook)
Subjects: LCSH: Earthmoving machinery–Juvenile literature. | Excavating machinery–Juvenile literature.
Classification: LCC TA725 .P48 2018 (print) | LCC TA725 (ebook) | DDC 629.225–dc23
LC record available at https://lccn.loc.gov/2016052742

Editor: Christina Leighton   Designer: Steve Porter

Printed in the United States of America, North Mankato, MN.

Table of **Contents**

MAKING NOISE

Earth movers are working at a **construction site**.

construction site

backhoe

One dumps dirt into a big truck.
Then it goes back for more dirt.

The earth movers are loud as they rip and dig up the earth.

Their powerful **diesel engines** are also noisy!

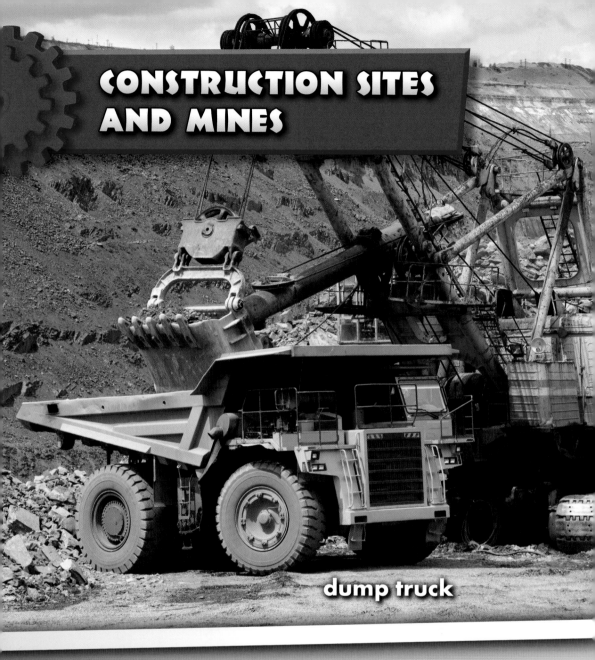

CONSTRUCTION SITES AND MINES

dump truck

There are many types of earth movers. Each has a different job.

Some of the machines push and **scoop** dirt. Others scrape and move it.

COMMON
EARTH MOVERS

dump truck

excavator

loader

scraper

Earth movers help with many construction jobs. They prepare land for buildings and roads.

THE LARGEST EARTH MOVER

P&H L-2350 Wheel Loader

height to cab: 22 feet (6.7 meters)

average human

length to bucket on ground: 66.5 feet (20.3 meters)

Some of the largest earth movers work at **mines**.

TIRES, TRACKS, BUCKETS, AND BLADES

These machines move with tires or **tracks**. Tires work best on hard ground.

grader

tires

bulldozer

tracks

Tracks keep the machines from sinking into soft ground.

Earth movers have different parts to help with certain jobs.

dump box

MACHINE PROFILE
BELAZ 75710 DUMP TRUCK

speed: 40 miles (64 kilometers) per hour

engines: two at 2,300 horsepower (1,715 kilowatts)

Some earth movers have **dump boxes**. These carry dirt from place to place.

Many earth movers have **buckets** that dig into the earth.

bucket ➞

excavator

These machines lift and move the dirt. They can make huge holes!

blade

Earth movers may have **blades**.
Some blades **level** the ground.

Other blades push dirt into piles. The blades may even scoop dirt into a **hopper**.

hopper

scraper

The different types of earth movers all work together.

They get the job done. Each day, earth movers work hard!

Glossary

blades—large metal plates that work like shovels

buckets—scoops on the ends of earth movers

construction site—a place where something is built

diesel engines—loud engines that burn diesel fuel and are often used in big machines

dump boxes—containers that hold the dump trucks' loads

hopper—the part of a scraper that holds the dirt

level—to make flat and even

mines—pits or tunnels from which materials are collected

scoop—to pick up and move

tracks—large belts that move in a loop around gears

To Learn More

AT THE LIBRARY

Allen, Kenny. *Earthmovers*. New York, N.Y.: Gareth Stevens Pub., 2013.

Bowman, Chris. *Backhoes*. Minneapolis, Minn.: Bellwether Media, 2017.

Doman, Mary Kate. *Earthmovers and Diggers*. Berkeley Heights, N.J.: Enslow Publishers, 2012.

ON THE WEB

Learning more about earth movers is as easy as 1, 2, 3.

1. Go to www.factsurfer.com.

2. Enter "earth movers" into the search box.

3. Click the "Surf" button and you will see a list of related web sites.

With factsurfer.com, finding more information is just a click away.

Index

The images in this book are reproduced through the courtesy of: Four Oaks, front cover; Dmitry Kalinovsky, pp. 4, 4-5, 6-7; dragunov, pp. 8-9; bondgrunge, p. 9 (dump truck); maggee, p. 9 (excavator); Valentin Valkov, p. 9 (loader); Nerthuz, p. 9 (scraper); Steve Porter, p. 10 (wheel loader graphic); buranatrakul, pp. 10-11; Budimir Jevtic, pp. 12-13 (grader); Mark Agnor, pp. 12-13 (bulldozer); Vladislav Gajic, pp. 14-15; LeitWolf, p. 15; rtem, p. 16; kaband, pp. 16-17; Deenida, pp. 18-19; Richard Thornton, p. 19; kurbanov, pp. 20-21.